BACON COOKBOOK

*Delicious Bacon Recipes
Simple Methods
Useful Tips
Common Mistakes*

By: Jason Goodfellow

© Copyright 2017 by Jason Goodfellow - All rights reserved.

This document is geared towards providing exact and reliable information in regards to the topic and issue covered. The publication is sold with the idea that the publisher is not required to render accounting, officially permitted, or otherwise, qualified services. If advice is necessary, legal or professional, a practiced individual in the profession should be ordered.

From a Declaration of Principles which was accepted and approved equally by a Committee of the American Bar Association and a Committee of Publishers and Associations.

In no way is it legal to reproduce, duplicate, or transmit any part of this document in either electronic means or in printed format. Recording of this publication is strictly prohibited and any storage of this document is not allowed unless with written permission from the publisher. All rights reserved.

The information provided herein is stated to be truthful and consistent, in that any liability, in terms of inattention or otherwise, by any usage or abuse of any policies, processes, or directions contained within is the solitary and utter responsibility of the recipient reader. Under no circumstances will any legal responsibility or blame be held against the publisher for any reparation, damages, or monetary loss due to the information herein, either directly or indirectly. Respective authors own all copyrights not held by the publisher. The information herein is offered for informational purposes solely, and is universal as so. The presentation of the information is without contract or any type of guarantee assurance.

The trademarks that are used are without any consent, and the publication of the trademark is without permission or backing by the trademark owner. All trademarks and brands within this book are for clarifying purposes only and are the owned by the owners themselves, not affiliated with this document.

Table of Contents

Introduction 1

Chapter One: You Can Bake Bacon? 3

Chapter Two: Benefits of Bacon from the Oven 6

1. Less grease...7

2. Crispier bacon...7

3. Less of a mess 7

4. More cooked at once 8

5. Diverse recipes..8

6. No curls...8

7. Still get that bacon frying smell in the house!.......9

Chapter Three: Equipment for the Job 10

- Oven 11

- Baking sheet 11

- Glazer (optional)...12

- Oven mitt 13

- Metal spatula 13

Chapter Four: How to Bake Satisfying Bacon (And How NOT to!) 15

How to Bake Bacon 16

Common Mistakes 17
- Putting bacon on oven racks directly 17
- Setting the heat too high 17
- Using the broiler setting instead of baking 18
- Leaving it in there too long 18
- Cooking it cold 19
- Overlapping and overcrowding 19
- Throwing out the leftover grease 20

Chapter Five: Keeping Your Oven Grease-Free 21
- Don't cover the bacon 22
- Catch the drippings 22
- Use a deep enough drip pan 23
- Try parchment paper and tin foil 24
- Keep the heat down 24

Chapter Six: Easy Tips for Beginner Bacon Bakers 26
- Watch carefully! 27
- Remember it will shrink while baking 27
- Plan ahead for time and batches 28
- Consider the thickness of your bacon 28
- Every oven is different 29
- Baking works for all types of bacon 29

Chapter Seven: Simple Recipes for Delicious Bacon Treats – From the Oven! 31

Maple Glazed Bacon 33

Brown Sugar Glazed Bacon 35

Pig Candy 37

Honey-Bourbon Glazed Bacon..............................39

Red Chili Glazed Bacon..41

Maple and Coffee Glazed Bacon............................43

Conclusion 45

Introduction

Have you ever wondered if there's a better way to cook your bacon? While it's sitting in the frying pan, spattering your whole stovetop and backsplash with oil, you're dreading the clean-up! But, it's better than just not eating bacon at all.

Actually, there's an easier way to cook bacon that won't cause half as much of a mess. Learn how to bake bacon! Maybe it doesn't sound quite right to you yet, but you'll soon find out that baking bacon is one of the best ways to get perfectly cooked bacon without suffering through the clean-up afterwards.

Learning how to bake bacon is easy and only takes a few dishes that you probably already have around your kitchen. The process takes no time at all to learn, and you can even make amazing bacon on your first try. You'll be able to sharpen your skills in no time and make it just the way you like time after time.

It's actually easier to get consistently good bacon once you know how to bake bacon. The oven can easily recreate the same type of bacon every time, whether you like it browned and crispy or soft and chewy. You can even cook glazed bacon recipes that will make your mouth water just reading them!

The sooner you learn how to bake bacon, the easier breakfast becomes, plus any other recipes that require bacon. So instead of suffering through dirtying your kitchen for some curled up bacon pieces, learn the secrets on how to bake bacon like a champ now.

Chapter One: You Can Bake Bacon?

In the US and some other parts of the world, bacon has become increasingly popular over the last decade. Its delicious taste and ability to blend seamlessly into a wide variety of dishes makes it the perfect kitchen companion for adding a little pizzazz to an otherwise boring dish. These days, you can find bacon lurking in everything from chocolates to salads and soup.

Even though it's in so many different recipes, cooking bacon has not undergone a lot of change over this time. Or, has it? It's always assumed that bacon should be placed in a pan and fried until it's just right, but that's not the only way to cook it. It can also be placed into the oven and baked until it's done. And no, I'm not talking about the microwave oven. Heating up your actual oven and baking bacon is one of the best ways to cook it, even though not a lot of people have figured that out yet.

There's a good chance that you and most of the people you know had no clue you can cook bacon in the oven. A misconception exists that you have to fry it to get it just right, but it's simply not true. You can make the perfect bacon, even better than fried in some opinions, by baking it instead of tossing it on the ol' frying pan.

Baked bacon will turn out largely the same as fried bacon, but the pieces will be straighter, crispier, and less greasy. Anything you would use fried bacon for, you can replace it with baked bacon. It is going to turn out well enough for any of the regular uses, and even give you a few more options than frying.

In reality, baking makes a lot of sense for bacon. After all, you can cook any kind of meat in the oven, right? It wouldn't be sensible to say that you can cook chicken or beef in the frying pan, but not in the oven, or vice versa. For that same reason, it doesn't make sense to say that bacon must only be cooked and prepared a certain way. Let's embrace the modern way to cook bacon in the oven, and learn how to get the best results from this new method!

Chapter Two: Benefits of Bacon from the Oven

Now that we've established that yes, you can cook bacon attitude, the next question to ask is; why? What makes baked bacon any better than fried or microwaved bacon? Actually, there are a lot of benefits to baking that can easily be summed up for you:

1. Less grease

To be clear about this point: the same amount of grease will be produced by the bacon when you're cooking it, but it won't set around on the food and get soaked up again. Instead, baking causes the grease to drip down to the pan below and leaves the bacon much less greasy as a result. Not only is this tastier and cleaner, it also makes your favorite food a bit healthier.

2. Crispier bacon

Although frying can yield some pretty good crisping for bacon, the oven can easily rival it. Plus, when you're baking; the entire piece will become crispy, not just the side that's touching the pan. Ovens can crisp bacon nicely even without all of the oils and fats that are needed for frying. So, the end result is a healthier and crispier piece of bacon for you to enjoy.

3. Less of a mess

One of the worst parts about frying bacon is the grease spattering. It tastes good in the end, but the mess that you then have to clean up from the pan, stovetop, counters, and backsplash are not always worth it. When you bake it instead, that grease doesn't end up all over the place. If you follow the right steps, it will all be contained within the pan and it won't even get around your oven at all.

4. More cooked at once

Ovens are way bigger than frying pans! So, you don't have to spend as much time doing multiple rounds of bacon on the pan. Instead, you can enjoy your time doing something else while you cook a much larger amount of bacon in the oven at once. Whenever you have a lot of cooking to do, it's easier to do it this way instead of doing multiple frying pans full.

5. Diverse recipes

When you're frying bacon, you don't have much control over what else you can do at that time. There is not much you can add to the meat, even if you really wanted to, because of the grease that could ruin most everything else in the pan.

Baking bacon gets rid of the monotony for you and allows you to try out a lot of new recipes. If you want to bake bacon, the basic recipe is very simple. But, it doesn't stop there. Other recipes abound that involve how to bake bacon in a clever way to incorporate it into a new dish or to give it some extra, delicious flavors.

6. No curls

Fried bacon can get some frustrating curls on the ends from the frying process. If you're preparing a nice recipe using bacon, it's best to have it in straight, more manageable pieces that won't curl up into a big mess.

Bacon does not curl while it's being cooked in the oven. Now you have a way to cook bacon and end up with long, straight pieces that are crispy and well cooked. No more curls on the edges, because the oven won't put them there. That is a problem exclusive to frying.

7. Still get that bacon frying smell in the house!

Don't worry, you won't lose the amazing smell of bacon cooking when you bake it instead of frying. We all love that smell that fills the house when you drop bacon slivers in a pan. Well, the same smell will also come from the oven as you're baking. Enjoy.

Chapter Three: Equipment for the Job

To get your bacon started in the oven, you'll only need a few everyday kitchen items. There's nothing fancy to do or any special gear you'll need. If you don't have any of these things, except the oven, you can easily borrow from a friend or spend a few bucks getting what's needed yourself.

Here are the supplies you'll want for baking bacon:

- Oven

The obvious first thing you'll need is a functional oven. It doesn't even matter how large of an oven it is, because that will only affect how much bacon you can make at once and won't mess with how well it cooks at all. The type of oven also doesn't matter. You can easily cook bacon in an electric or a gas oven without problem, as long as it can reach the right temperature and maintain it for the necessary time.

If you don't have a full conventional oven, you can use a small toaster oven. The size and power of the oven isn't going to affect how the bacon will be cooked or not, assuming it can reach the right temperature range. Toaster ovens are actually very convenient for bacon, because they are smaller and can heat up more quickly than a conventional oven. This means you can make your breakfast bacon faster in the mornings and have your meal done quickly.

- Baking sheet

To place the bacon in the oven, you'll need a baking sheet that's properly fitting into your oven. It's possible to use all different kinds of baking sheets, including cooking sheets, but I would recommend looking for one that allows the grease to drip off the bacon. If you use a flat cookie sheet, the grease will still be sitting around the bacon the whole time. While you can still do this, it's better to try a combination of pans or a different type.

Broiler pans are very useful in this capacity, because they have a top piece with slats that allow the grease to drip down into a metal collection tray. This is ideal to make the bacon less greasy and keep it healthier. Beyond the health benefit, the lack of grease also helps it to keep its shape and get crispier more quickly.

If you don't have an actual broiling pan, you can simulate the affect by placing an oven-safe metal drying rack onto a flat cookie sheet. The bacon will then lay on top of the drying rack, allowing grease to drip away as its cooking. This works equally as well as a broiling pan, so you can do whichever method is most easily available to you.

- Glazer (optional)

Many people prefer glazing their bacon when baking it in the oven. If you want to do that and follow any of the recipes that I'm going to list later on, you may need a simple glazing brush to apply the ingredients onto your bacon. However, if you just want to cook bacon straight up, you won't need a glazer to get it done.

- Oven mitt

Another more obvious thing you'll need is an oven mitt. To place the tray in the oven and remove it, you'll need something to protect you from the heat. A simple heat resistant oven mitt will do the trick, nothing fancy is needed!

- Metal spatula

Bacon will sometimes need to be turned over while you're cooking it. So that you can do this easily, have a long enough metal spatula ready for your use. You don't want to make it a big hassle by pulling the tray out, rotating the bacon, and then continuing. Instead, use a long spatula or tongs to rotate them while it's still in the oven to keep things simpler.

All the items I listed here are open for substitutions. You don't have to do things exactly with the same equipment as I do to have a successful batch of bacon come out. The only thing you need to do is make sure you follow the directions as best as you can. You can use something similar enough as long as the main purpose is accomplished.

As I mentioned earlier, you don't even really need a traditional oven to bake bacon, as long as you have a toaster oven or something similar that can reach and maintain the right temperatures. Similarly, you don't need to use a specific type of pan, although it's recommended that you use something that will allow the bacon grease to drip away from the bacon itself. Other than these two factors, there's nothing else you have to keep constant. You can do as you please and be creative if you wish!

I'm a firm believer in creativity in the kitchen. If you want to follow the recipe exactly to get the exact results that it specifies, that's fine. However, if you want to try something a little different, that's also completely okay. Food is flexible, and cooking should never be boring.

Chapter Four: How to Bake Satisfying Bacon (And How NOT to!)

Here I'm going to show you how you can use all your equipment and finally get your bacon started in the oven. The basic recipe here is very simple. There are very few steps and even fewer ingredients (hint: bacon.), so you can try it out any time you're ready.

How to Bake Bacon

1. Turn your oven on and let it pre-heat to 400 degrees Fahrenheit.

2. If you're using a cookie sheet and metal drying rack, place the rack on top of the cookie sheet and lay the bacon slices out on top of the rack. If you're using a broiling pan, put it together and lay the bacon out on top. Make sure the bacon slices aren't overlapping, or else they won't cook evenly.

3. Place your baking tray into the oven and allow it to cook for 10 – 15 minutes. At this time, you should check on the bacon and see how well it's cooking. Those that like their bacon crispier can leave it in the oven for an extra 10 minutes, but if you like it softer then you should remove it after the first 15 minutes.

4. The bacon is now done cooking. To remove any excess oils and fats from the bacon, you can place it on a plate covered with paper towels. This will help to soak up any remaining grease and oil to leave you with crispy, healthier bacon slices.

See? It's simple! Just 4 quick steps and you'll have your tasty bacon ready to go. This is the most basic recipe for baking bacon. Anyone can do it and get the benefits of baked bacon.

Even though it's an easy recipe, there are a few things you can do to accidentally mess it up. To help you avoid any potential problems, I want to go over some of the most common mistakes made when baking bacon. Check it out and save yourself from the trouble later on.

Common Mistakes

- Putting bacon on oven racks directly

Although you could lay the bacon on the interior oven racks directly and keep a tray underneath for the drippings, this probably isn't a great idea. You're going to create a big, greasy mess in your oven. Plus, what might be on the racks already from previous meals? Oven racks are rarely cleaned in most households, so it would be a mistake to assume they're clean unless you just cleaned them thoroughly yourself. Overall, this is a move you should only do as a last resort.

- Setting the heat too high

Bacon can go from crispy to burnt too quickly to catch sometimes. If you want to avoid this, make sure the heat level is correct. Cooking bacon the right way may take a few extra minutes, but you'll be almost sure of not burning it. If you turn the temperature up too high, it's more likely that it will burn if you don't pay attention to it constantly.

- Using the broiler setting instead of baking

Most ovens have a few different cooking modes. The normal ovens bakes, but there is also a setting called broiling. This setting turns on a high-powered heating element on the top of the oven that is great for adding a nice crisp layer on top of a steak or casserole. However, it's also a sure-fire way to burn your bacon.

The problem is that this heating element is going to get too hot too quickly. Also, it's a concentrated heat that doesn't circulate around the oven as much and focusing on cooking from the top down. Both of those are recipes for a disastrous baked bacon!

- Leaving it in there too long

The crispier the better, right? I love crispy bacon as much as the next person, but that doesn't mean you can leave it in the oven for a long time just to make it better. The maximum you should ever leave it in a hot oven is about 25 minutes. Even that might be too long, and you may risk burning it at that time. Check it after 15 minutes, but definitely remove it at 25 minutes or you'll risk overcooking it and having a burnt mess instead of a nice crunch.

One of the problems with bacon that you might not realize is that it won't stop cooking just because you remove it from the oven. Bacon is a very fatty meat, and fat does not cool down instantly. Instead, the bacon fat will keep cooking for a few minutes while it's cooling. So, if you cook the bacon too long, it could end up getting overcooked even after you've removed it from the oven!

- Cooking it cold

Another interesting fact about bacon is that the fat causes it to cook differently than other meats. Bacon meat is primarily fat, and fat does not cook well when it's cool or cold. If you want evenly cooked bacon that all turns out about the same, you should let your bacon reach room temperature before cooking it.

That means if you want to cook bacon, take it out of the fridge about 15 minutes before it's time to put it in the oven. You can actually remove it from the fridge when you start pre-heating the oven, and by the time the oven is heated it will most likely be warm enough to cook properly.

- Overlapping and overcrowding

If you crowd your bacon on the rack or tray, you will risk it cooking unevenly and poorly. I know it's tempting to just throw the last few remaining slices on the rack so you can get it all down at once, but that's not really the best way to make a good batch of bacon. This is especially true if your bacon is overlapping at any point on the rack.

Overlapping causes the pieces to become thicker in some areas and thinner in others. Two slices on top of each other won't cook at the same rate or in the same way that one slice alone will. So, laying slices even partly over each other will make those pieces a uneven and inconsistent with the rest of the bacon in the oven.

- Throwing out the leftover grease

Okay, so this one isn't necessarily a mistake that you make when cooking. But, keeping your leftover bacon fat drippings is a great way to enhance a lot of other meals you might be cooking soon. Bacon grease can be used to cook all kinds of things, including vegetables and even cookies!

To save the grease, all you have to do is let the baking tray cool down a little bit, then strain the grease into a glass jar. Close the jar and leave it in the fridge. The grease will harden in the fridge, but will melt again when exposed to heat for cooking.

Chapter Five: Keeping Your Oven Grease-Free

We know that when you're frying bacon the grease pops and gets everywhere around the stovetop. Luckily, the oven method makes a much smaller mess. When you're baking bacon, the grease doesn't pop everywhere inside the oven. That's a big advantage in terms of cleaning up your mess! But, there are a few ways you can make it even easier to clean up. Who wouldn't want to make cleaning up easier than normal?

- Don't cover the bacon

It may seem counterintuitive, but bacon in the oven really doesn't need to be covered at all! It will only slow down the cooking and mess up the timing, possibly even cooking the bacon a bit wrong. This may not be a tip to make cleaning up easier, but it will make it easier for you to get the bacon ready and to cook it. There's no point in covering the bacon, since the grease will not start popping around anyway.

- Catch the drippings

The biggest mess that happens with bacon in the oven is the grease dripping down. It's essential that you use a drip tray or pan underneath the wire drying rack or broiler your bacon is cooking on! If you fail to use a pan or tray to catch the dripping grease, you'll end up with an enormous mess all over your oven that will be really difficult to clean, and potentially a safety hazard.

Another issue that can come from grease drippings is smoke. If grease escapes into the open oven or touches one of the bottom heating elements, it can create a lot of smoke. That is something you really don't want to deal with, especially when you'll be in the kitchen cooking!

The bottom line here is that you absolutely need something oven-safe to catch all the grease drippings. Remember that you're dealing with bacon, so the drippings will be pretty extensive!

- Use a deep enough drip pan

Now that you know you have to use a pan to catch the drippings, it's a good idea to also know that your pan of choice has to be deep enough for all the drippings. Bacon is primarily made up of fat, which means that a lot of that fat is going to cook off and drip down in the form of grease.

If you don't have a deep enough pan to deal with all the grease, it might overflow while cooking or while you're removing it from the oven. Either way, the result would be a big mess that you shouldn't have to deal with! Avoid the mess entirely by using a deep pan depending on how much bacon you want to cook at once. Also, you can use a pan that's wider in area than the cooling rack, which will help to spread the grease out instead of letting it pool up and spill over quickly.

In order to have an effective pan, you need to make sure you're not using a warped or bent metal tray or pan for grease drippings. Some thinner baking sheets can get warped by high temperatures, or have just gotten worn down over time. If this is the case, you may notice the liquid grease pooling up on the lower side and eventually spilling over the edge. What a disaster! Choose a flat, un-warped pan instead.

- Try parchment paper and tin foil

A lot of people who make bacon in the oven recommend using tin foil inside your baking sheet to make it easier to dispose of the mess. The foil will cover the pan and collect all the drippings without the pan even having to touch the grease. In other words, covering the pan with foil before you put your bacon in will mean not having to wash the pan afterwards.

Other recipes recommend putting parchment paper inside the tin foil that collects drippings. This trick helps to absorb the fats and grease, so there's much less of a chance of it spilling out at any point during the cooking or when you're removing the tray. Parchment paper isn't a necessity, especially if you plan to save the bacon grease for other mealtimes, but it's a good idea for a simpler cleanup.

- Keep the heat down

If you heat up the oven too much to try to make your bacon cook faster or become crispier, you will risk making the grease start popping and ensure that you don't make the same mistake in your oven.

Keeping the heat to the recommended lower temperature will also reduce the amount of smoke that comes from cooking the bacon. Sometimes it's possible to accidentally smoke up the kitchen a bit when you turn up the heat too much, but lowering the heat will help to avoid any smoke. 400 degrees Fahrenheit is the hottest that you should bake bacon at, but you can go as low as 350 degrees and still manage to cook it well. Lower temperatures will take longer to bake it, but the results will be largely the same.

Chapter Six: Easy Tips for Beginner Bacon Bakers

Although baking bacon is a simple recipe, it might be quite difficult if you haven't really had any experience cooking before! So, if you're a beginner or even an experienced cook that wants a bit of a refresher, here are some great tips to keep in mind for baking bacon:

- Watch carefully!

If you've never cooked bacon before, you may not be aware that bacon can go from done to burnt in a matter of seconds. The only way to make sure it doesn't burn is to keep an eye on it when it's nearly done. You can tell when the bacon goes from soggy and flat to crispy. But, slightly crispy isn't what everyone likes. Those that like bacon extra crispy will want to carefully watch the bacon once it's started to crisp.

Burnt bacon is no good, so you're going to have to be vigilant to keep it from getting to this point. Remember the tip I mentioned earlier that bacon may continue to cook a little after it's done, because of the hot fat. It's better to underdo it than overdo it, because you can always put it back in the oven if it's not completely done, but you can't un-burn it!

- Remember it will shrink while baking

Bacon generally loses some of its size, no matter how you're cooking it. This is completely normal, and you shouldn't be surprised to find smaller cooked strips than the raw strips you started with. Make these assumptions if you're planning it to serve your guests or if you need the bacon for a recipe. Most people prefer to buy large slices so that they end up with pretty decent pieces once the cooking is finished as well.

- Plan ahead for time and batches

Baking your bacon is a great way to save time in preparation, as long as you plan enough ahead. It will take some time to preheat the oven, and the baking itself takes a minimum of 10 – 15 minutes. But, the good news is that you can cook multiple batches at once and can do pretty large batches on each tray.

It's usually safe to assume the first batch will take around 30 minutes, because of preheating. Any subsequent batches can take as little as 15 minutes, depending on what your oven is like and how you prefer your bacon.

Another thing to consider is that the bacon might cook differently depending on how you place the batches in the oven. Placing them too close to each other on the racks may cause them to cook more slowly. Putting too many cooking trays in at once may also cause slower cooking, although it might be worth it to get it all done at once. Just check each rack as they're cooking, because they may finish at different times.

- Consider the thickness of your bacon

Thicker bacon pieces cook more slowly than thin pieces. If you're baking thin bacon slices, you won't need to leave the tray in the oven for nearly as long as for thick bacon slices. Although you'll get pretty consistent results if you use the same type of bacon over and over again, different thickness really impacts the cooking time.

- Every oven is different

Ovens do not all have the same power levels. More powerful ovens will generally cook bacon faster than less powerful ovens. If you have a more powerful oven, keep a closer watch on your bacon, as it may actually be done sooner than you expect.

Different ovens can also circulate air in different ways. Air circulation accounts for the even cooking that happens in an oven. Without good circulation, your bacon could end up a bit uneven and you may need to flip it over while it's cooking. This isn't very likely, but it's something to keep a lookout for anyway to make sure you're mastering your oven to create the best batch of bacon possible.

- Baking works for all types of bacon

If you don't eat regular pork bacon for any reason, don't worry. You can also cook other types of bacon in the oven, including the most popular alternative, turkey bacon. The recipe and method will be essentially the same, except some people like to season their bacon alternatives before baking them. The results should be the same as when you cook regular bacon.

All these tips and more will help you get the best results from your bacon cooking. Baking is the easiest and arguably the cleanest way to cook bacon without making it too limp or flabby. If you're a fan of crisp, flat bacon then you should try cooking it in the oven. Follow the steps and take any tips to heart if they might help you out, and your bacon should end up exactly how you like it.

Chapter Seven: Simple Recipes for Delicious Bacon Treats – From the Oven!

Feeling a bit more creative? There are lots of other ways you can enhance your bacon when you make it in the oven. You don't have to settle for regular bacon if you're feeling a little more adventurous. Here are a few of my favorite recipes for baked bacon.

Maple Glazed Bacon

This recipe is sweet and salty at the same time. It's a good little treat that you can enjoy after your meal or with a few drinks. Be careful though, it can definitely turn out sticky!

1. Set up your bacon as if you were going to bake it plain. Pre-heat the oven at 400 degrees Fahrenheit.

2. Place the baking sheet with bacon into the oven. Let it cook alone for about 15 – 20 minutes to allow it to begin browning. Once it starts browning, take out the bacon. Using a glazing brush, lightly brush each slice of bacon with 100% pure maple syrup.

3. Return the tray to the oven and let it bake for another 3 – 5 minutes. After this time, it should turn to a warm golden brown color. Take it out of the oven and move the bacon to a plate with paper towels. Serve as usual.

Tip: Higher quality maple syrup will make this recipe better than low-quality maple syrup. The better the syrup, the better the results of this glazing will be. Choose a good, 100% pure maple syrup from a trusted brand.

Brown Sugar Glazed Bacon

Brown sugar glazed is another very simple recipe for easy glazing. All you need is two ingredients, and it takes the same amount of time as baking plain bacon. This glaze adds a sweet touch to an otherwise salty food, so it can be enjoyed in even more ways.

1. Pre-heat your oven to 400 degrees Fahrenheit.

2. Arrange your bacon on a tray as you would for plain baked bacon.

3. Sprinkle brown sugar evenly over each piece of bacon. Put the tray in the oven and bake it for 15 – 18 minutes. Remove when it is crisp and appears nicely glazed.

4. Shift bacon to a plate with paper towels and allow it to cool a little bit before serving.

Tip: Brown sugar glazed bacon is best served when there aren't a lot of other sweet elements to the meals. It's not a great choice for a pancake breakfast, but it works great with eggs and your morning coffee instead.

Pig Candy

Here is a simple recipe for an easy crowd pleaser that has a pretty sophisticated taste. Only 4 ingredients are needed, but the end result is simultaneously sweet, salty, and a little spicy.

1. Gather your ingredients: ½ cup of brown sugar, ¼ teaspoon of cayenne pepper, 1 pound of bacon, and 1 tablespoon of sherry vinegar.

2. Toss the brown sugar and cayenne pepper together in a small bowl and put it to the side.

3. Arrange the bacon for the oven as you would normally.

4. Brush bacon with the sherry vinegar and sprinkle on the sugar and cayenne mixture. Put it in the oven and bake for 10 minutes.

5. After 10 minutes, turn the trays around to make sure they are cooking evenly. Wait 5 more minutes and begin to check for doneness.

6. This recipe will be done when the bacon is starting to crisp and the strips are a nice dark brown color. Remove it from the oven and put it on a cooling rack over paper towels. Serve when cooled.

Tip: You can prepare this before a party or event and it will hold up with full flavor for hours at room temperature.

Honey-Bourbon Glazed Bacon

Here is a nice recipe that has a bit more of a bite to it. The Bourbon mixes nicely with the sweet ingredients to create a rich and delightful snack.

1. Gather your ingredients: ¼ cup clover honey, 2 tablespoons high quality bourbon whiskey, 12 slices

of thick cut double-smoked bacon, and coarsely ground black pepper.

2. Preheat the oven to 350 degree Fahrenheit. This is cooler than normal for bacon, but that's because you are trying to avoid burning any of the glaze ingredients while cooking.

3. Arrange the bacon as you normally would for baking. Bake for 10 minutes.

4. While it's baking, combine honey and bourbon together in a sauce pan or small pot and allow it to heat to a boil. Remove from the heat and let it cool a little bit, but not all the way.

5. Remove the bacon from the oven and brush it with the honey bourbon mixture. Return the bacon to the oven for another 10 – 15 minutes and allow the mixture to caramelize in the oven. Remove when it starts getting crispy and dark colored. Sprinkle with black pepper and serve.

Tip: For crispier bacon, leave it in a little longer. But be careful, it can quickly turn from crisp to burnt with this glaze.

Red Chili Glazed Bacon

While similar to the brown sugar glazed bacon, this recipe adds a nice kick of spice to the taste. This turns it from a regular dessert bacon to a nice accompaniment for a cocktail, salad, or a general snack.

1. Gather your ingredients: 12 slices of apple wood smoked thick cut bacon, ¼ cup of brown sugar, salt, pepper, and 1 tablespoon of crushed dried red chilies. (you can substitute with red pepper flakes)

2. Pre-heat the oven to 350 degrees Fahrenheit.

3. Arrange your bacon on wire racks as you would for regular baking. Sprinkle it with the brown sugar, salt, black pepper, and crushed red chilies.

4. Place the tray in the oven and bake for around 20 minutes until it is crisp. Remove from the oven and place on a plate with paper towels. Serve when ready.

Tip: You can also make this recipe by placing the bacon directly onto the parchment-lined baking sheet. This will cook some of the oils into the other spices to make it a smoother glaze. However, it will also make it messier and keep more grease on the bacon.

Maple and Coffee Glazed Bacon

If maple syrup glazed bacon sounds a bit too plain and you want something more interesting, this espresso-based glaze adds a fantastic touch to a classic glaze recipe.

1. Gather your ingredients: 1 shot of espresso, 12 slices of thick cut smoky bacon, 1 tablespoon of maple syrup, and 2 tablespoons of dark brown sugar.

2. Preheat the oven to 350 degrees Fahrenheit.

3. Set up your bacon as you would for regular baking.

4. In a bowl to the side, combine the espresso, maple syrup, and dark brown sugar. Mix it together until the sugar is mostly dissolved and well combined.

5. Brush the mixture onto each bacon slice with a glazing brush. Save half of the glaze for later. Place the glazed bacon slices into the oven.

6. Bake the bacon for 10 minutes. Then, remove it from the oven. Increase the heat to 400 degrees Fahrenheit.

7. Flip each piece of bacon over with a set of metal tongs. Brush the remaining glaze over the other half of the bacon and return it to the oven for another 10 – 15 minutes until it's crisp and caramelized.

8. Cool before serving for best results.

Tip: This is a good snack to make for a brunch or as a treat with for a get-together. Even though it has coffee flavoring, it goes really well with coffee or tea any time of the day.

Conclusion

Baking bacon is a great way to end up with perfectly cooking bacon that doesn't leave such a huge mess. Frying pans can give you good results, but it takes a lot more work to get it just right. The microwave suits some people, but the results are usually less than pleasing for most people. Ovens create the best environment for bacon to cook exactly like you want it to, and to be consistent.

Read over the tips given in this book about how to bake the best bacon, and check back any time if you need a refresher. Happy cooking!

Once again, thank you for buying this book and good luck.

Regards, Jason Goodfellow

Printed in Great Britain
by Amazon